WHAT THE BANKS ASK & WHY

WHAT THE BANKS ASK & WHY

Everything You Need to Know
before Applying for a Mortgage
If You're Self-Employed or
Have a Complex Income

Robert Moffat

BA, MLIBF, DipFA, DipMAP, CeRER, CertLTCP, CeMAP

For more information, contact:
whatthebanksaskandwhy@mail.com

FIRST EDITION

Paperback ISBN: 978-1-80227-712-8
eBook ISBN: 978-1-80227-713-5

Table of Contents

Who is this book for?

"How long will it take and how much will it cost?" was the most common question I would get asked. With all applications, without exception, clients wanted to know the payment terms and how quickly the money could be made available. In the past 2-3 years, however, that has been overtaken with a sense of frustration and confusion as people ask, "Why is the bank asking for that? Why does it matter to them?!"

This book explains, in detail, what questions mortgage lenders ask and why. It explains the importance of ensuring your mortgage application is 100% accurate. It shows how giving the underwriter the most comprehensive understanding of your finances and ability to repay the mortgage is the best way to get your application approved and a mortgage offer issued as quickly as possible.

This book demonstrates the value of getting an experienced mortgage broker who is familiar with the challenges of self-employed/complex income cases and, more importantly, has a good relationship with lenders involved in that market. Some lenders are considerably better than others for self-employed or people with complex income structures.

Why the Interest Rate Matters

Unless you are buying with cash, the purchase price you pay for a property, whether it's £250,000 or £2.5M, is not the true cost of the house. The true cost is the total you pay back to the bank, plus your deposit…

There are many factors which impact on the interest rate you will be offered by a lender. This includes everything from the Loan to Value you apply for, your credit history, the type of property you are buying and your personal/financial circumstances. What you want, in all cases, is the lowest interest rate you can get for the longest period of time. The last ten years have seen some of the lowest mortgage interest rates ever offered. However, over the last 30-40 years, interest rates have been much higher. The lower the interest rate, the less you will pay back to the lender over the term of the mortgage. Even a 0.5% or 1% difference in interest rates can have a monumental impact on the amount of money you will pay the bank over the term of the mortgage.

Purchase Price			Deposit			Mortgage			Term		
£250,000			£62,500			£187,500			25 Years		
Interest Rate	Monthly Payment	Total to Pay Over 25 Years	Interest Rate	Monthly Payment	Total to Pay Over 25 Years	Interest Rate	Monthly Payment	Total to Pay Over 25 Years	Interest Rate	Monthly Payment	Total to Pay Over 25 Years
1%	£707	£274,491	2%	£795	£300,918	3%	£889	£329,244	4%	£990	£359,408

Purchase Price			Deposit			Mortgage			Term		
£500,000			£125,000			£375,000			25 Years		
Interest Rate	Monthly Payment	Total to Pay Over 25 Years	Interest Rate	Monthly Payment	Total to Pay Over 25 Years	Interest Rate	Monthly Payment	Total to Pay Over 25 Years	Interest Rate	Monthly Payment	Total to Pay Over 25 Years
1%	£1,413	£548,982	2%	£1,589	£601,836	3%	£1,778	£658,488	4%	£1,979	£718,816

Purchase Price			Deposit			Mortgage			Term		
£750,000			£187,500			£562,500			25 Years		
Interest Rate	Monthly Payment	Total to Pay Over 25 Years	Interest Rate	Monthly Payment	Total to Pay Over 25 Years	Interest Rate	Monthly Payment	Total to Pay Over 25 Years	Interest Rate	Monthly Payment	Total to Pay Over 25 Years
1%	£2,120	£823,472	2%	£2,384	£902,754	3%	£2,667	£987,732	4%	£2,969	£1,078,225

Purchase Price			Deposit			Mortgage			Term		
£1,000,000			£250,000			£750,000			25 Years		
Interest Rate	Monthly Payment	Total to Pay Over 25 Years	Interest Rate	Monthly Payment	Total to Pay Over 25 Years	Interest Rate	Monthly Payment	Total to Pay Over 25 Years	Interest Rate	Monthly Payment	Total to Pay Over 25 Years
1%	£2,827	£1,097,963	2%	£3,179	£1,203,672	3%	£3,557	£1,316,975	4%	£3,959	£1,437,633

Purchase Price			Deposit			Mortgage			Term		
£1,500,000			£375,000			£1,125,000			25 Years		
Interest Rate	Monthly Payment	Total to Pay Over 25 Years	Interest Rate	Monthly Payment	Total to Pay Over 25 Years	Interest Rate	Monthly Payment	Total to Pay Over 25 Years	Interest Rate	Monthly Payment	Total to Pay Over 25 Years
1%	£4,240	£1,646,945	2%	£4,768	£1,805,508	3%	£5,335	£1,975,463	4%	£5,938	£2,156,449

Purchase Price			Deposit			Mortgage			Term		
£2,000,000			£500,000			£1,500,000			25 Years		
Interest Rate	Monthly Payment	Total to Pay Over 25 Years	Interest Rate	Monthly Payment	Total to Pay Over 25 Years	Interest Rate	Monthly Payment	Total to Pay Over 25 Years	Interest Rate	Monthly Payment	Total to Pay Over 25 Years
1%	£5,653	£2,195,926	2%	£6,358	£2,407,345	3%	£7,113	£2,633,951	4%	£7,918	£2,875,266

Purchase Price			Deposit			Mortgage			Term		
£2,500,000			£625,000			£1,875,000			25 Years		
Interest Rate	Monthly Payment	Total to Pay Over 25 Years	Interest Rate	Monthly Payment	Total to Pay Over 25 Years	Interest Rate	Monthly Payment	Total to Pay Over 25 Years	Interest Rate	Monthly Payment	Total to Pay Over 25 Years
1%	£7,066	£2,744,908	2%	£7,947	£3,009,181	3%	£8,891	£3,292,439	4%	£9,897	£3,594,082

Why the Mortgage Term Matters

Unless you are buying with cash, the purchase price you pay for a property, whether it's £250,000 or £2.5M, is not the true cost of the house. The true cost is the total you pay back to the bank, plus your deposit… Lenders charge interest on the amount you borrow from them; every year you have their money, you pay them interest. Logically, the longer you have their money, the more interest you pay. This can mean the actual cost of buying the house can vary significantly, depending on how long you decide to borrow for. People are often tempted to borrow over the longest possible term, as this results in the lowest monthly payments. However, this leads to paying back much more interest to the lender over the duration of the mortgage.

Purchase Price	Deposit	Mortgage	Interest Rate
£250,000	£62,500	£187,500	3%

Mortgage Term	Monthly Payment	Total To Pay Over Mortgage Term (Including Deposit)
5 Years	£3,369.13	£264,648
10 Years	£1,810.51	£279,762
15 Years	£1,294.84	£295,571
20 Years	£1,039.87	£312,069
25 Years	£889.15	£329,244
30 Years	£790.51	£347,083
35 Years	£721.59	£365,570
40 Years	£671.22	£384,686

Purchase Price	Deposit	Mortgage	Interest Rate
£500,000	£125,000	£375,000	3%

Mortgage Term	Monthly Payment	Total To Pay Over Mortgage Term (Including Deposit)
5 Years	£6,738.26	£529,296
10 Years	£3,621.03	£559,523
15 Years	£2,589.68	£591,143
20 Years	£2,079.74	£624,138
25 Years	£1,778.29	£658,488
30 Years	£1,581.02	£694,165
35 Years	£1,443.19	£731,139
40 Years	£1,342.44	£769,372

Purchase Price	Deposit	Mortgage	Interest Rate
£750,000	£187,500	£562,500	3%

Mortgage Term	Monthly Payment	Total To Pay Over Mortgage Term (Including Deposit)
5 Years	£10,107.39	£793,943
10 Years	£5,431.54	£839,285
15 Years	£3,884.52	£886,714
20 Years	£3,119.61	£936,207
25 Years	£2,667.44	£987,732
30 Years	£2,371.52	£1,041,248
35 Years	£2,164.78	£1,096,709
40 Years	£2,013.66	£1,154,058

Purchase Price	Deposit	Mortgage	Interest Rate
£1,000,000	£250,000	£750,000	3%

Mortgage Term	Monthly Payment	Total To Pay Over Mortgage Term (Including Deposit)
5 Years	£13,476.52	£1,058,591
10 Years	£7,242.06	£1,119,047
15 Years	£5,179.36	£1,182,285
20 Years	£4,159.48	£1,248,276
25 Years	£3,556.58	£1,316,975
30 Years	£3,162.03	£1,388,331
35 Years	£2,886.38	£1,462,278
40 Years	£2,684.88	£1,538,744

Purchase Price	Deposit	Mortgage	Interest Rate
£1,500,000	£375,000	£1,125,000	3%

Mortgage Term	Monthly Payment	Total To Pay Over Mortgage Term (Including Deposit)
5 Years	£20,214.78	£1,587,887
10 Years	£10,863.08	£1,678,570
15 Years	£7,769.04	£1,773,428
20 Years	£6,239.22	£1,872,414
25 Years	£5,334.88	£1,975,463
30 Years	£4,743.05	£2,082,496
35 Years	£4,329.56	£2,193,417
40 Years	£4,027.32	£2,308,116

Purchase Price	Deposit	Mortgage	Interest Rate
£2,000,000	£500,000	£1,500,000	3%

Mortgage Term	Monthly Payment	Total To Pay Over Mortgage Term (Including Deposit)
5 Years	£26,953.04	£2,117,182
10 Years	£14,484.11	£2,238,093
15 Years	£10,358.72	£2,364,570
20 Years	£8,318.96	£2,496,551
25 Years	£7,113.17	£2,633,951
30 Years	£6,324.06	£2,776,662
35 Years	£5,772.75	£2,924,556
40 Years	£5,369.77	£3,077,488

Purchase Price	Deposit	Mortgage	Interest Rate
£2,500,000	£625,000	£1,875,000	3%

Mortgage Term	Monthly Payment	Total To Pay Over Mortgage Term (Including Deposit)
5 Years	£33,691.29	£2,646,478
10 Years	£18,105.14	£2,797,617
15 Years	£12,948.41	£2,955,713
20 Years	£10,398.70	£3,120,689
25 Years	£8,891.46	£3,292,439
30 Years	£7,905.08	£3,470,827
35 Years	£7,215.94	£3,655,695
40 Years	£6,712.21	£3,846,860

Employment/Company Structures & How Lenders Assess Income

Different types of structure
Partnership/Limited Liability Partnership
What figure(s) does the lender use to calculate income?
Share of Net Profit/ Drawings from Business
What different ways can they calculate the "total income" to be used in the affordability calculation?
Latest Tax Year End Or Average of last 2 Tax Year Ends Or Average of last 3 Tax Year Ends
What documents will lenders require to verify income?
1-3 Years' Partnership Accounts Accountants Reference/Letter from accountant 1-3 Years' SA302s/Tax Calculations 1-3 Years' Corresponding Tax Year Overviews Personal Bank Statements Business Bank Statements

Employment/Company Structures & How Lenders Assess Income

Different types of structure
Limited Company
What figure(s) does the lender use to calculate income?
Salary + Dividends (From Company Financial Year End) Or Salary + Dividends (From Tax Year End) Or Salary + Share of Profit Before Corporation Tax (From Company Financial Year End) Or Salary + Share of Profit After Corporation Tax (From Company Financial Year End)
What different ways can they calculate the "total income" to be used in the affordability calculation?
Latest Financial Year End Or Average of last 2 Financial Year Ends Or Average of last 3 Financial Year Ends Latest Tax Year End Or Average of last 2 Tax Year Ends Or Average of last 3 Tax Year Ends
What documents will lenders require to verify income?
1-3 Years' Ltd Company Accounts Accountants Reference/Letter from accountant 1-3 Years' SA302s/Tax Calculations 1-3 Years' Corresponding Tax Year Overviews Personal Bank Statements Business Bank Statements

Employment/Company Structures & How Lenders Assess Income

Different types of structure
Holding or Parent Company with one subsidiary trading company
What figure(s) does the lender use to calculate income?
Salary (From Trading Company) + Dividends (From Parent Company) Or Salary (From Trading Company) + Share of Profit Before Corporation Tax (From Parent Company) Or Salary (From Trading Company) + Share of Profit After Corporation Tax (From Parent Company)
What different ways can they calculate the "total income" to be used in the affordability calculation?
Latest Financial Year End Or Average of last 2 Financial Year Ends Or Average of last 3 Financial Year Ends Or Latest Tax Year End Or Average of last 2 Tax Year Ends Or Average of last 3 Tax Year Ends
What documents will lenders require to verify income?
1-3 Years' Ltd Company Accounts (Parent Company & Trading Company) Accountants Reference/ Letter from accountant 1-3 Years' SA302s/Tax Calculations 1-3 Years' Corresponding Tax Year Overviews Personal Bank Statements Business Bank Statements

Employment/Company Structures & How Lenders Assess Income

Different types of structure
Holding or Parent Company with multiple subsidiary trading companies
What figure(s) does the lender use to calculate income?
Salary (From Trading Companies) + Dividends (From Parent Company) Or Salary (From Trading Companies) + Share of Profit Before Corporation Tax (From Parent Company) Or Salary (From Trading Companies) + Share of Profit After Corporation Tax (From Parent Company)
What different ways can they calculate the "total income" to be used in the affordability calculation?
Latest Financial Year End Or Average of last 2 Financial Year Ends Or Average of last 3 Financial Year Ends Or Latest Tax Year End Or Average of last 2 Tax Year Ends Or Average of last 3 Tax Year Ends
What documents will lenders require to verify income?
1-3 Years Ltd Company Accounts (Parent Company & Trading Companies) Accountants Reference/ Letter from accountant 1-3 Years SA302's/Tax Calculations 1-3 Years Corresponding Tax Year Overviews Personal Bank Statements Business Bank Statements

What other income/additional income will a lender take into consideration?
➢ Attendance Allowance ➢ Carer's Allowance ➢ Child Benefit ➢ Child Tax Credit ➢ Disability Living Allowance ➢ Employment & Support Allowance ➢ Injuries Disablement Benefit ➢ Investment Income ➢ Maintenance Income ➢ Pension Income ➢ Rental Income ➢ Trust Fund Income.
What is the maximum a lender will lend based on "total income"?
From 3.5x income to a maximum of 6x Total Income **Many other factors will impact the maximum mortgage deemed affordable, e.g. credit commitments, living expenses, private school fees and child/adult dependants**
What impact do different lenders' ways of assessing income have on how much you can borrow?
How a lender calculates your annual income + Whether that lender uses a 1/2/3-year average + What maximum income multiple a lender will use = A massive variance of borrowing power from one lender to the next. Identical mortgage applications could result in different lenders offering a maximum mortgage of hundreds of thousands or millions of pounds. Making sure your mortgage application is with the right lender for your present and future circumstances is important. Consider if you may wish to borrow more or move home in the future before locking into a long-term rate with a lender who might not be able to help you when the time comes.

Here is an example of how the same income can lead to different maximum loan amounts with different lenders.		
Husband & Wife Are Both Shareholders in a Family Business (Equal Shareholding) Financial Year End December 2021 Share of Profit Before Corporation Tax – £750,000 Each Financial Year End December 2021 Share of Profit After Corporation – Tax £607,500 Each Salary Tax Year Ending April 2022 – £12,500 Each Dividends Tax Year Ending April 2022 – £100,000 Each Financial Year End December 2020 Share of Profit Before Corporation Tax – £500,000 Each Financial Year End December 2020 Share of Profit After Corporation Tax – £405,000 Each Salary Tax Year Ending April 2021 – £10,000 Each Dividends Tax Year Ending April 2021 – £75,000 Each ... Financial Year End December 2019 Share of Profit Before Corporation Tax – £250,000 Each Financial Year End December 2019 Share of Profit After Corporation Tax – £202,500 Each Salary Tax Year Ending April 2020 – £8,000 Each Dividends Tax Year Ending April 2020 – £50,000 Each		
Cautions Lender – Maximum Mortgage (Before Accounting for Financial Outgoings)	Balance Lender – Maximum Mortgage (Before Accounting for Financial Outgoings)	Adventurous Lender – Maximum Mortgage (Before Accounting for Financial Outgoings)
Average of Salary & Dividends for Both Applicants Over 3 Years X 3.5 = £596,167 Max Mortgage	Most Recent Year Salary + Most Recent Share of Profit After Corporation Tax For Both Applicants X 5.49 = £6,807,600 Max Mortgage	Most Recent Year Salary + Most Recent Share of Profit Before Corporation Tax For Both Applicants X 6 = £9,150,000 Max Mortgage
Same Clients, Same Income, Different Lenders. Over £8.5M swing from the lowest maximum mortgage to the highest maximum mortgage. Getting your mortgage application to the most suitable lender for your personal financial circumstances matters. Expert advice matters		

Chapter 1

The Basics/ Personal Details

What the Banks Ask For

- ✓ Full Name, Including any Middle Names
- ✓ Date of Birth
- ✓ Country & Town of Birth
- ✓ Maiden Name
- ✓ Mother's Maiden Name
- ✓ Marital Status
- ✓ Date Married
- ✓ National Insurance Number
- ✓ Planned Retirement Age
- ✓ Length of Time Living in the United Kingdom
- ✓ Citizenship
- ✓ Permanent Right to Reside in the UK
- ✓ Email Address
- ✓ Mobile Phone Number
- ✓ Home Phone Number
- ✓ Work Phone Number

Why Banks Ask

The majority of personal information lenders ask for as part of your mortgage application is self-explanatory; however, not getting this 100% accurate from the outset can seriously delay your house purchase or remortgage further down the line. Lenders make certain assumptions unless explicitly told otherwise – so it's important to get the basics correct.

Full Name Including any Middle Names & Date of Birth: The mortgage loan is secured on the property you are buying or refinancing. The title deeds to that property will be in your name and must match the mortgage application and standard security/mortgage deed. Missing out a middle name on a mortgage application might not be picked up straight away but will delay matters when the case reaches the legal work being completed at the end. Your full name and date of birth are also crucial as the lender will run a full credit search.

Country & Town of Birth: Lenders will use this as a standard security question if you ever call them to discuss your mortgage in the future, for example, to make an overpayment. However, it also triggers additional questions if you confirm you were born outside of the UK.

Marital Status: Most lenders require married applicants to have a joint mortgage; very few allow only one applicant to own the house and hold the mortgage if the spouse also lives in the house. This is for several reasons, but primarily due to their concerns that the spouse not on the mortgage has issues with either adverse credit history or is trying to hide some other problem from the lender (such as untaxed income, benefit fraud, etc.). Lenders will ask the date you were married and, for female applicants, the date your name was changed along with your maiden name – this is so they can credit search both your current and previous names from the outset. In some cases, if you've been married but not updated documents like a driver's license, passports, proof of address, or utility bills, this can slow things down. Lenders may ask for a certified copy of your marriage certificate.

National Insurance Number: Lenders want to confirm your National Insurance Number matches the payslips, P60s, Tax Returns and other documents provided to them. Lenders can also use this to speak with HMRC and ensure that the employment history you have declared matches what the Inland Revenue knows. This helps lenders identify fraudulent applications. Lenders also reserve the right to ask for statements of earnings from HMRC for previous years to identify any spikes in income.

Planned Retirement Age: Lenders will generally assume your planned retirement age is the state pension age unless you tell them otherwise. There are several lenders who will lend until age 70, 75 and even 80 if you are in a non-manual job and declare you intend to keep working until that age. Equally, if you tell a lender you intend to retire at age 55, then either your mortgage term needs to finish before you turn 55, or you have to prove you will have sufficient income in retirement to keep up with the mortgage payments.

You should think exceptionally hard about taking a mortgage term past the age you will realistically bc ablc to work. Interest rates have been low for a long time but are currently increasing and likely will continue to return to the mean in the coming years. If you cannot afford the mortgage over a sensible period of 20-25 years, finishing before you turn 70 at the latest, you should seriously consider buying a cheaper house that you can afford both now and in the future.

Length of Time Living in The United Kingdom/Citizenship & Permanent Rights to Reside: Lenders' criteria on these three issues varies wildly from one bank to the next. Some lenders are OK with foreign nationals, people who have been in the UK less than three years or do not yet have permanent rights to reside, and other lenders take a very hard-line view on this. Even people from the EU require proof they have been granted settled status before applying for a mortgage with some banks. Lenders will ask for copies of passports, visas, permanent right to reside and other documentation as part of the application. Ultimately their concern is giving a 25-year mortgage to someone who only has two years left on their visa.

Basic Contact Details: Lenders insist on accurate contact information for several reasons. Your email address allows them to email copies of your mortgage offer and other documents to you directly and, with most lenders, facilitates access to manage your mortgage online (make overpayments, view the balance, etc.). Correct mobile and employer phone numbers protect against identity theft and mortgage fraud. It allows the lender to contact you if needed to discuss your application. Nothing looks more suspicious to a lender than somebody who doesn't want to tell them their phone number or email address. Lenders will, on occasion, call your employer to verify that you work there, your remuneration package and how long you have been employed.

Chapter 2

Proof of Identity & Proof of Address

What the Banks Ask For

- ✓ Current Address/Postcode
- ✓ Date Moved in
- ✓ Tenure (Owner, Rented, Living with family)
- ✓ Previous address history for a minimum of 3-6 years
- ✓ Driver's License Number/Registered Postcode/Expiry Date
- ✓ Passport Number/Expiry Date

Why Banks Ask

Address History: Lenders look for at least 3-6 years of address history. It's essential you provide each address you lived at during that time, as lenders will run a credit search at each property to ensure there are no missed or late payments not being disclosed. Lenders will ask whether you owned the property or rented it. With the latter, they will look for proof of address in the form of council tax or utility bills). In cases where you were living with family, it can be harder to provide proof of address. In these situations, it's important that your driving licence and bank statements are registered to the correct residence.

Drivers Licence: Lenders regularly want a copy of your photo driving licence as one form of proof of identity to be submitted as part of your application. They also usually want your driving licence number and the postcode your licence is registered to keyed into the application form. This helps speed up their ID & AML (Anti-Money Laundering) checks. It is important that your licence is in date and registered at the correct address.

Passport: Lenders also often want a copy of your passport as a secondary proof of identity to be submitted as part of your application. They also regularly want your passport number keyed into the application form. This, again, helps speed up their ID & AML (Anti-Money Laundering) checks. It is important your passport is valid and in date. The passport also confirms citizenship. If any other country than the UK is shown, the lender will then ask for copies of any visa and/or permanent right to reside documentation.

Chapter 3

Child Dependants, Adult Dependants & Other Occupiers

What the Banks Ask For

- ✓ Full Name & Date of Birth of Anyone Else Living in the Property
- ✓ Details of any Dependants Living Elsewhere that You Are Financially Responsible for

Why Banks Ask

Lenders want to know about every single person who is or will be living in the property. Sometimes, that will affect how much they'll be prepared to lend. In other cases, it will determine what paperwork or additional paperwork needs to be signed. This can cause significant delays if things aren't disclosed on the application from the outset, so it's really important to get this information to the lender as part of the application for several reasons. Most importantly, you don't want to look like you're hiding information because lenders take a very dim view of that. Secondary, you don't want things delayed when it gets to the solicitors' stage and are then having to get additional paperwork signed and dealt with at the 11th hour – especially if this needs to be sent back to the lender for approval.

Obviously, the most common question is if you have dependent children. Any kids under the age of 18 need to be disclosed because the lender will view them as a dependant, which will impact how much you can borrow and how much is affordable. So, if you're on £100K a year household income, that's maybe giving you a maximum mortgage of £550,000, for example. Having one or two kids isn't going to have a massive impact on that; for some lenders, it won't have any impact at all. However, if you've got ten kids, that's obviously quite an expense on a monthly basis, and they're going to look to lend much less as a result of that. Anywhere in between, be it 3, 4, 5, 6 or 7 kids, will affect how much you can borrow from the lender.

There are two things that can help mitigate any reduction in maximum loan due to having child dependants. The first is an additional income such as child benefit, child tax credit, or explaining to a lender you have no childcare costs as you work from home or have family who look after the kids during the day. The second is if any of the kids are 16/17 years old, have left school or work full-time. Some lenders can remove them as "dependants" if they are not financially dependent on the applicants.

You also need to disclose any adult dependants. They could be elderly relatives or somebody else who is living on the property. Now they won't always have an impact on affordability because they might have their own source of income, which might be pension income or benefit income, or they are financially self-sufficient. If they are not financially dependent on you, that's not as much of an issue for a lender, but it certainly must be disclosed. Any adult aged 18 or over living in the property, even if not financially dependent, must be disclosed to the lender. Often, these are adult kids over the age of 18 who are working full-time, have their own income and are effectively self-sufficient. They're maybe just waiting to move out or saving for a deposit. That's totally fine; it won't impact at all on how much you can borrow.

The reason all people over the age of 18 must be disclosed to the lender (regardless of being financially dependent or not!) is that they will have to sign what's called a "consent to mortgage" form. Effectively, when you take out a mortgage, you are telling the bank you are borrowing X amount. You are going to repay it, but if you don't, the lender will repossess the property. At that point, you and anybody else who is named on the mortgage will obviously be kicked out of the house, and the house will be repossessed and sold. Anybody else living in the property at that time over the age of 18 would also be evicted. So the lender requires a "consent to mortgage" form if anybody over the age of 18 lives in the property. They have to sign this form which basically says that in the event of a repossession (as unlikely as that is), they would also be out. Despite not being named on the mortgage nor having any responsibilities to pay it, in the event of a repossession, they would be homeless at that point.

If you have any adult dependants you are responsible for; even if they live at a separate address, then the lender will use this information to reduce how much you can potentially borrow. This could be sending £500 a month to a child who is at university and living away from home. Or it could be paying the living costs of an elderly relative on a fixed income who needs to be financially supported. It's important to factor these commitments in from the outset to ensure the right lender is chosen from day one. There is not much point in going to a lender who will say yes initially, then see the bank statements and the associated expenditure and then reduce the amount they will lend below the threshold you need.

Chapter 4

Employment History & Business Interests

What the Banks Ask For

- ✓ Employment Type
- ✓ Full/Part-Time
- ✓ What Industry Do You Work in
- ✓ Job Title
- ✓ Employer Name
- ✓ Employer Address/Postcode
- ✓ Employer Phone Number
- ✓ Start Date of Employment
- ✓ Owner/Director of Business
- ✓ % Shareholding of the Business
- ✓ Gross Annual Income
- ✓ Previous Year Annual Income
- ✓ Details of any Wage Rises/Promotions in the Past 12 Months

✓ If the Business Has Been Restructured in the Past Five Years, Provide Full Details
✓ Previous Employment if in Current Company/Role less than 12 Full Months
✓ Details in any/all Businesses You Have an Interest or Shareholding in

Why Banks Ask

The source and proof of your income is the most important part of your mortgage application. There is a real common misconception that lenders look at "3 months of payslips for employed applicants and 3 years of accounts for self-employed applicants," and that's it. Nothing could be further from the truth. Lenders ask an inordinate number of questions about an applicant's income as part of a mortgage application. They are making a decision to lend hundreds of thousands/millions of pounds over a 25-40-year time frame, and that lender wants to be absolutely certain of your ability to repay the mortgage.

Employment Type: Most applicants in the UK fall into one of two main categories: either a full-time employee of a business and have no shares in the business at all, or are "self-employed" where they are the director and 100% owner of a Limited Company. However, for the people who don't fall into these categories, it can feel like a real challenge to get a mortgage. Contractors, Employees of Family Businesses, Minority Shareholders and owners of recently restructured businesses need expert advice to make sure they apply to the best lender for their circumstances.

Employment History: Lenders look for a consistent income year on year and often need a minimum of three months' payslips and the latest one or two years' P60s to prove income. Lenders look at year-to-date figures on the payslip to ensure there has been no spike in income preceding the mortgage application. For example, if you are on £120,000 gross per annum, that's £10,000 per month, so seven months into the tax year, the "Year-To-Date" figure for gross pay should be £70,000. If it is less, then the lender knows you have not been on this income for long. If it is much less, this is a red flag to the lender that your income has increased dramatically in the months prior to applying for a mortgage.

Recent Change of Employment or Income: People move jobs regularly and often for an increased wage. Lenders have no problem with this in principle, as long as the change is plausible and realistic. For example, a manager of a logistics company on £100,000 per year moving to a Haulage company for £120,000 per annum is within reason. Moving from an administrative role on £30,000 per year to a senior management position on £90,000 per year is simply not plausible for the lender, especially if that move directly precedes a mortgage application. Lenders are fighting incredibly hard (and rightfully so!) to stamp out mortgage fraud within the industry. The most common is "staged income," where applicants artificially increase their wages for 3-6 months, apply for a large mortgage, and then reduce their wages back down after securing it.

For this reason, lenders are exceptionally cautious of applications where people work for family-owned businesses, as these are where the majority of staged income applications came from. Getting a natural pay increase or promotion is fine, and wage increases of 5%-20% (varies by lender) are considered acceptable. However, large spikes in salary are simply not permissible as lenders believe this is a short-term artificial increase. There are plenty of legitimate reasons for an increase, such as the end of a probation period or natural career progression and promotion, and those cases will be considered carefully by lenders. Cases where income has increased from £60,000 to £100,000, then three months later, a mortgage application goes in for £550,000 (exactly 5.5 times the new salary) are likely to be robustly declined by lenders.

In cases where there has been an increase, it certainly helps to submit a letter from the company accountant. For example, it may be that the turnover has gone from £1,000,000 to £5,000,000 to £10,000,000 in five years. As the business is expanding, it's now a case of more people coming on board, and they're coming in with decent salaries to continue to grow the company. If it's plausible and the accountant can provide that information/explanation, it can be the difference between a case being approved or declined. There are lots of industries that are doing very well at the moment and are paying their staff good wages to get the right people into the business. If there has been any wage increase, it's vitally important that when the application is submitted to the lender, a letter is included with the application from the outset explaining the circumstances to the underwriter. For example, if the applicant has gone from being a national sales manager to being responsible for all of Asia.

Another common example is due to companies changing from office-based work to "working from home." It has allowed people in Glasgow to work for London-based companies (paying twice the salary for similar roles) because they do not physically need to be in the office. It's all about how plausible and sustainable the underwriter believes the income to be.

Age vs. Industry vs. Income: Lenders have quite sophisticated technology, which automatically flags information that doesn't seem plausible or within normal parameters. This doesn't mean the lender will decline the case, just that they will require more information – and it looks much better to provide that explanation upfront along with the application. For example, a project manager earning £200,000 a year in their 40s is something a lender probably wouldn't look twice at. However, somebody at 18 earning that same money is the type of thing that a lender will question and say – well, what's going on here? That doesn't seem plausible. Do they work for a family business, how long have they earned that amount of money etc.? In some cases, professional sports players and athletes and people in certain industries can earn an astronomical amount of money at a very young age. Yet, generally speaking, lenders expect to see figures in line with certain parameters.

Income Structure (Employed): Lenders all have different ways of assessing employed income. The split between Salary/Overtime/Commission/Monthly Bonus/Annual Bonus can significantly impact on how much you can borrow. In some cases, different lenders average the income of 3-12 months' payslips. If your income is a low basic salary and a high bonus or commission, it's even more important to go to a lender who specialises in these cases. A check that some lenders do is to match the surnames of the applicant to all the directors and shareholders of the business that the applicant works for. If it appears there is any connection, additional information and documents will be requested to ensure the income declared on the application is legitimate.

Income Structure (Self-Employed): Regardless of whether you own 1% or 100% of a business, some lenders will view your income from the perspective of being self-employed. They look at Salary, Dividends and Share of Profit Before/After Corporation Tax. They look at the previous three years' accounts and, in some cases, require a projection or management accounts along with business bank statements for the current financial year. Approaching the correct lender for your personal financial circumstances is paramount. How much someone can borrow can vary by hundreds of thousands, sometimes millions of pounds, depending on how the individual lender assesses the income. This becomes even more complicated when there has been a recent restructure (e.g. from a partnership to a limited company, or from a simple trading company to a layered company structure or holding company with trading subsidiaries). Any such changes need to be explained clearly to an underwriter (ideally via a letter from the company accountant). The underwriter needs to know that the income you can draw is sufficient to pay the mortgage and is sustainable for potentially the next 20+ years.

Documents to Prove Income: Lenders have complete discretion to ask for as much or as little documentation as they feel necessary to verify your income. This will vary from lender to lender and from case to case, but generally speaking, you should be prepared to provide the following.

Employed Income	Self-Employed Income
➢ 3-12 Months' payslips ➢ 1 or 2 Years' P60(s) ➢ Personal Bank Statements	➢ 1-3 Years' Company Accounts ➢ Accountants Reference/Letter from accountant. ➢ 1-3 Years' SA302s/Tax Calculations ➢ 1-3 Years' Corresponding Tax Year Overviews ➢ Personal Bank Statements ➢ Business Bank Statements

Technology Available to Lenders: Mortgage lenders have developed their own and have access to 3rd party software to enable them to identify and prevent mortgage fraud. These sophisticated systems are not overtly described here in any detail because, by their very nature, they are used to prevent mortgage fraud, so publishing information/details on how they work would not be well received! The moral of the story is misrepresenting information on a mortgage application is fraud. There is no middle ground, and there are no varying degrees of severity as far as mortgage lenders are concerned. Lenders share data on mortgage applications, so if you go to one lender and say you are self-employed and then six months later go to a different lender and say you are a full-time employee, that sets off alarm bells. Lenders keep records of staged income applications, including complicit businesses. Therefore, if one person gets a pay rise for three months, gets a mortgage and then their income miraculously reduces after the mortgage is completed, every single person who works for that company could have their application scrutinised for years to come regardless of which lender they go to. Artificially increasing wages for the purpose of obtaining a mortgage is Mortgage Fraud – it always has been. The only difference now is lenders have the technology to spot it a mile away.

Lenders will continue to share information back and forwards with HMRC. As your income is linked to your National Insurance number, it's not hard for lenders to be alerted to spikes and subsequent declines in income pre/post mortgage application. Lenders have the ability to search through online filed company house documents. If they find out you have shares in the business (or the parent company, holding company or family trust that owns the trading business) that were not disclosed on the application, that will likely lead to the mortgage offer being delayed or, indeed, the case getting declined. The advice is to go to a mortgage adviser who specialises in mortgages for those with self-employed or complex incomes and get your mortgage with the most suitable lender from the outset. Do not try and hammer a square peg into a round hole, and do not try and misrepresent the facts of your case to a lender. Instead, go to the right mortgage broker, and place your case with the right lender from the outset.

There are several lenders who specialise in mortgages for people who are self-employed or have a complex income and who do not deal directly with borrowers. The only way to get a mortgage with one of these lenders is via a broker on their approved panel; you cannot apply to them directly.

Chapter 5

Accountants Details

What the Banks Ask For

- ✓ Firm of Accountants
- ✓ Accountant Name
- ✓ Account Address/Postcode
- ✓ Accountant's Phone Number
- ✓ Accountant's Email Address
- ✓ How Long the Accountants Have Acted for You
- ✓ Accountant's Qualifications
- ✓ Previous Accountants if Acted for Less than Three Years

Why Banks Ask

Lenders will use certain documents to assess and verify your income. These include company accounts, SA100s (Full Tax Return) and Tax Calculations with corresponding Tax Year Overviews. These documents will usually be considered valid by lenders for a maximum of 18 months.

Financial Accounts for the financial year ending December 2022 would be considered valid until 30th June 2024, for example.

Tax Returns for Tax Year Ending 5th April 2022 would be considered valid until 5th October 2023, for example.

As a result of these documents being potentially over a year old by the time you apply for a mortgage, the lender often wishes to see things like business bank statements that show a turnover consistent with the proof of income documents provided.

Lenders may ask for a projection from the company accountant, or, in more complex cases, they may wish to see management accounts for the business's current trading year. Lenders rely on accountants to give them an honest overview of the company. They ultimately want to be satisfied that the income taken from the business is sustainable for the term of the mortgage.

Depending on the size of the business, there may be several accountancy firms involved:

- Accountants for the company/companies
- Auditors for the company/companies
- Accountants for preparing tax returns for the individual directors/shareholders

It's important to provide a detailed explanation to the lender on which firm has which responsibilities. Therefore, if further information or an accountant's reference is needed, it can be requested from the correct person quickly to avoid any unnecessary delays.

Lenders want to know how long your accountants have acted for you, and if there have been any changes in the past three years, they will want to know who the previous accountants were too. This is because if your current accountant has only been acting for the business for two months, they are unlikely to be able or willing to comment on the previous three years' accounts.

A letter from the accountant can go a long way to giving the underwriter some comfort that your application should be approved and that, ultimately, you're going to be able to draw an income for the next 10, 15, or 20 years out of that company. Every lender/underwriter reserves the right to ask for supporting information/documents regarding your mortgage application. Some lenders will ask for copies of the full accounts, and some will be happy with an accountant's reference, which will typically confirm the following details on a 1-2-page document:

- Name & Company Number of Parent Company/Holding Company, if applicable
- Name & Company Number of Trading Company/Companies
- Business Address
- Industry/Nature of Business
- Date Business Established
- Applicant 1 & Applicant 2 Percentage Shareholding
- Financial Data for the Latest 2-3 Years, such as:
  - Annual Turnover
  - Gross Profit
  - Operating Profit Before/After Corporation Tax
  - Applicant 1/Applicant 2 Salary
  - Applicant 1/Applicant 2 Dividends
  - Retained Profits (After Dividends Paid)
  - Balance Sheet Info Such as Assets, Liabilities, Director's Loans & Capital Account
- Commentary on how the business is doing and any reason for a sharp increase/decrease in turnover/profit from one year to the next. Depending on the industry, the accountant may be asked specific questions with regards to how the business navigated Covid, Brexit and other external factors.

Chapter 6

Solicitor's Details

What the Banks Ask For

- ✓ Firm of Solicitors
- ✓ Firm Address/Postcode
- ✓ Name of Solicitor Handling the Transaction
- ✓ Contact Number & Email Address of the Solicitor Handling the Transaction

Why Banks Ask

When buying a property, there is a considerable amount of legal work and legal paperwork to be completed. In almost all purchases, your solicitor will act for both you and the lender.

The mortgage loan funds will be sent to your solicitor, who will combine this with your deposit funds and send these to the sellers on the date of completion.

The solicitors will prepare and have you sign the standard security/mortgage deed.

In almost all cases, your solicitor will be on the lender's approved panel of solicitors. Most solicitors who do residential conveyancing are on most lenders' panels; it's difficult to be in the industry of residential conveyancing if you can only deal with a small number of lenders. Most lenders have similar criteria, and they want there to be at least two or three partners within the firm. They look for them to be trading for a certain number of years before being allowed to act for them in transactions. The reason for this is relatively simple: residential conveyancers deal with hundreds of millions of pounds of lenders' money every day. Therefore, lenders need to make sure their money is in safe hands for the (albeit brief) period they are in control of the lender's money.

For whatever reason, if your solicitors are not on your chosen lender's panel, you can do one of two things. You can get another firm of solicitors to act instead (for both you and the bank), or you can keep your firm of solicitors to act for you and pay for another firm of solicitors to act for the bank. This is called separate representation, and it routinely increases the cost and timescale of a transaction being completed.

It's essential to get the details right in terms of address and email address because that's how the lender is going to communicate with that solicitor. That's where they're going to send the mortgage offer, all the paperwork to be signed, including the standard security or mortgage deed.

Chapter 7

Property Details

What the Banks Ask For

- ✓ Address & Postcode of Property
- ✓ Purchase Price
- ✓ Purchase Date
- ✓ Current Expected Valuation
- ✓ Property Type
- ✓ Number of Bedrooms
- ✓ Number of Bathrooms
- ✓ Number of Living Rooms
- ✓ Number of Kitchens
- ✓ Year Property Built
- ✓ Wall Type
- ✓ Roof Type
- ✓ Number of Garages/Parking Spaces
- ✓ Standard Construction
- ✓ Commercial Adjacent
- ✓ Any Improvements Made to the Property Since Purchase

Why Banks Ask

Generally speaking, most properties are considered suitable for mortgages for most lenders, but by no means are all properties suitable for all lenders.

Lenders look for a standard list of information on the property when the application is submitted before making any type of decision on whether to lend. Some of these are quite self-intuitive, but with others, people wonder why does that matter? Why does the bank care?

Location: This covers the basics like the address and postcode of the property. If it's a purchase, they want to see that it's in the same area as you're living in now. If it's far away, they like to look for an explanation as to why that is. For example, if you are currently living and working in Edinburgh and want to buy a six-bed house in Coventry, they're going to want to know why that is. Why are you moving? Also, what's the situation with your employment? Are you taking a new job down there? In which case, they're going to look for those details. Or will you continue working for the same company and work remotely? Do you work from home, or does the company you work for have offices in other parts of the UK? That's all vital information to a lender; they want to know why you're buying a property where you are.

Expected Valuation: What do you think the house is going to be worth? This is especially important in markets that are very, very busy and where people are paying well over the true value for the property. So, if you're buying a house that's valued at £500,000, but you're paying £600,000, effectively, that 100K difference is coming out of your own pocket. You're spending that money yourself. The lender is not going to lend based on a figure that is more than the property is worth. Hence, it's essential to know what the house is worth, not just what you're paying for it. Even if the lender valued it for mortgage purposes at £600,000 today – that does not guarantee you could achieve the same sales price in the future.

They also require basic details like the number of bedrooms, bathrooms, living rooms, kitchens etc. They want to have a good understanding of the type of property you're buying, and they're looking for that to be plausible based on your circumstances. If you're a single person buying a six-bed house, that is going to raise some questions. They're going to want to know whether there's maybe a spouse or partner in the background and why they are not being included on the application. The lender will question if there are kids that perhaps haven't been disclosed on the application.

Property Construction: The lender wants to know about all aspects of the property, starting with the age of the property. When buying a property that is 200+ years old, it's not uncommon for lenders to request a structural engineer's report, a damp report or another specialist report to confirm the property is suitable to secure a mortgage against. Things like wall type and roof type are important, as not all type of construction is considered suitable by all lenders. Things like steel-framed construction and concrete construction aren't acceptable to all lenders. Therefore, it's essential to know what type of construction a property is and if it's going to require any specialist surveys or structural engineers reports to be submitted to the lender. Sometimes it can be easier to choose a different lender who, as standard, accepts that type of construction as opposed to one who only accepts that type of construction along with a specialist report from an engineer.

Commercial Adjacent: If the property is near or above any type of commercial property, that can affect which lender will be suitable.

Whether it's right beside an industrial unit, a shop, a petrol station or any kind of commercial premises, it can impact whether a lender chooses to lend on that property, so it's important to determine that before applying for the mortgage. The one frustrating thing for borrowers is that lenders often say, "suitable subject to valuers comments," which basically means they will send out a local surveyor picked at random from their approved panel. That surveyor will have to comment on things like saleability, i.e. would the lenders have any issues or delays selling the property in the event of a repossession? One surveyor might say yes, and another might say no.

Number of Acres of Land: Most lenders have a maximum number of acres that can come with a property. For example, with many high street banks, you can buy a property that has up to three acres, but they won't lend if there are any more than three acres. Other lenders will go up to ten acres, but if it comes with more than ten acres, they'll consider it a commercial property and won't lend anything. The number of acres coming with a property is very important to know at the outset. How much land is coming with the property you're buying? If you're also buying land separately as part of a separate transaction, the lender wants to know that, and that's essential information to determine which lender to go to. Most lenders require you to advise if you are buying land adjacent to the property, even as part of a separate transaction on a different date.

Property Improvements (Remortgage): One of the things that some lenders ask for (and for the lenders who don't ask, you should tell them anyway) is the details of any improvements made to the property since purchasing it. When you're remortgaging a property that you're already living in, it can be very helpful to let the lender know any improvements you've made to that property. These may include new kitchens, bathrooms, additional living space, changing things like double glazing, improving the central heating system and converting the loft. Any improvements to the value of the property could result in a lender giving you a better interest rate on your remortgage. The more equity there is in a property, the more the property is valued, and the better interest rate you're likely to get on that remortgage.

In recent months, lenders have started offering mortgages with lower rates and cash back on properties with an A/B/C EPC rating. This is to reward and encourage people to make their homes as environmentally friendly as possible.

Property Improvements (Purchase): One of the major causes of delay in buying/selling a property in the UK is not having the correct paperwork for building work such as Extensions, Loft Conversions etc. People regularly get Planning Permission/Building Warrant, then carry out the work without getting the completion certificate from the council. If the proper paperwork is not in place, the property could be valued at zero until the paperwork has been retrospectively granted. This is a slow and often costly process. It can take up to six months to get a retrospective completion certificate or letter of comfort. If you're buying a property and it looks like it's been extended or improved/had building work done, you must make sure that your solicitor is asking the seller's solicitor for the paperwork (Planning Permission, Building Warrant, Completion Certificate etc.) the day you make your offer. It's important to remember your solicitor will never see the inside of your house. Therefore, you have to be proactive and tell them to request this paperwork or at least confirm with the seller's solicitors that it's not needed to avoid any unnecessary delays).

Valuations: There are different types of valuations for mortgage purposes. Getting a full internal valuation done can take several weeks depending on the availability of the local surveyors, then another 2-3 days to get the valuation report back. To counter this delay, lenders are trying to use technology to reduce the number of cases that require a full valuation. This is another reason it's vital to give accurate property details to the lender. If they value it at less than you expect, it will almost always result in a worse interest rate being offered.

AVMs (Automated Valuation Model): The lender's internal systems determine the value of the property based on the information available (including the original purchase price and recent local sold prices).

Desktop Valuations: A local surveyor looks at the property from their office (including the original purchase price and using recent local sold price information, location information via google maps and other proprietary software) and decides on the value of the property.

Drive-by Valuations: A local surveyor views the property from the outside only and combines this with recently sold price information/ proprietary software to make a decision on the value of the property.

Full/Internal Valuation: A local surveyor will make arrangements to view the property inside and out and then decide on its value.

Chapter 8

Current Mortgage Details

What the Banks Ask

- ✓ Current Mortgage Lender
- ✓ Current Mortgage Balance
- ✓ Current Mortgage Term
- ✓ Current Mortgage Interest Rate
- ✓ Current Mortgage Payment
- ✓ Current Mortgage Account Number
- ✓ Current Mortgage Structure
- ✓ Current Early Repayment Charge

Why Banks Ask

Remortgage Applications: Lenders need the details of your current mortgage for practical reasons. Your new mortgage is going to repay your old one, and lenders will usually appoint a firm of free solicitors to handle the switch. Details such as your current mortgage balance, lender name, mortgage account number and whether your mortgage is in one part or has multiple subaccounts are all important. Getting this information correct at the outset will avoid delays further down the line. If you are raising additional funds (remortgage for a higher amount than your current balance,) the lender requires full details of the new loan funds.

Purchase Applications: Lenders need the details of your current lender to make it a condition of your new mortgage that your old one is repaid in full. (If for whatever reason, you do not plan to repay your current mortgage because you intend to keep your current house and rent it out as a Buy-To-Let, then that must be declared to the lender from the outset). Lenders are also looking at how you manage your finances from the standpoint of your current mortgage. For example, if you have a £375,000 mortgage and want to buy a much larger house and borrow £750,000, then lenders look at how you are currently managing things like loans, credit cards etc. If you are nearly maxed out on your credit card, that is a warning sign to a lender that if your mortgage debt (and payments!) were doubled, it might push you into financial hardship.

Chapter 9

Credit Commitments & Credit History

What the Banks Ask

- ✓ Whose Credit Commitment is it? (Applicant 1 or 2)
- ✓ Type of Commitment? (Loan, Credit Card, Car Finance, Buy Now Pay Later)
- ✓ Who is the Provider?
- ✓ What is the Current Balance?
- ✓ What is the Credit Limit?
- ✓ What is the Interest Rate?
- ✓ Are You Planning to Pay it off Within Three Months?
- ✓ What is the Monthly Payment?
- ✓ In the Last Six Years, have You Missed a Payment on a Credit Agreement, had a Default, CCJ, or Been in Arrears with Borrowing?
- ✓ Have You Ever Been Bankrupt, Had a Property Repossessed or Been in a Debt Management Plan or Trust Deed?

Why Banks Ask

This is one of the most important parts of a mortgage application and one of the main factors in determining which lenders will be available and what interest rate you are likely to be given. Applicants with better credit scores and better credit histories generally get lower mortgage interest rates.

Lenders are going to make a decision on whether to lend hundreds of thousands/millions of pounds to you based on what you have done with credit in the past. They are looking at things such as: Have you paid it on time? Have you taken it out and used it responsibly? Banks can make a lot of determinations about your future payment conduct from what you've done in, say, the last four, five or six years. They will do a credit search as standard, and it's not just the credit score that they're interested in. It's the actual underlying data they're looking at: what type of credit you've had in the past, be it mortgages, car finance, loans, overdrafts, store cards etc. They're looking for that money to have been used responsibly and paid on time over the last four, five or six years, as that's a very important indicator to lenders of how you will act in the future.

They're also looking at things like what's your available credit. It doesn't matter whether you've got a credit card with a £1000 limit; if you're up at £900 or £950 on it, that's using 90 to 95% of your available credit, which is very, very poorly looked at. That's actually looked at far worse than somebody who potentially has a £20,000 credit limit but is only using £10,000. Although that's a much higher number, it's a much lower percentage. They want to know that when you've got credit, you're not using every single penny available. If you're using every single penny of available credit, you don't have anything left if you need the money in an emergency situation or at short notice. And people who are already running up credit card balances are looked upon very poorly by lenders when they're applying for mortgage finance.

They will also look at when you've opened credit accounts. If you've opened a lot within a short space of time, that can be seen as a warning sign to lenders regarding you being financially over-committed each month. Let's say you have a very, very good credit rating and never missed any payments, but a month ago, you took out a Land Rover at £900 a month and, two months ago, a Jaguar at £1000 a month. In month three, you're applying for a £900,000 mortgage. The lender might take the view that, actually, although you've had a good credit history in the past and you paid everything on time, you are spiking massively. Your monthly payments are going from very little to a huge amount in a very short space of time. So if you are going to go and take out a large car or another type of credit agreement, you have two options. You could get your mortgage first; that way, it's not an issue, or apply for your mortgage maybe three, four or five months further down the line. This means you can show that you've had that new payment, e.g. car finance, that the new agreement has been paid on time, there have been no issues, and it's not had any impact on your other finances or ability to pay things on time.

One of the most common things that delays an application is a small default or missed payments that people haven't even been aware of. For example, a mobile phone contract that's come to the end of the term and hasn't been cancelled properly, or a gas or utility bill from a previous property and you didn't realise there was a final payment due on the account when you moved out.

The amount of times that a small default or a CCJ appears on a credit file is more common than people think. So lenders won't decline an application just because there has been a missed payment, a CCJ, or a default. It's about explaining to a lender, what happened, why it happened, when it happened and more importantly, that you fixed it as soon as it came to your attention. If you've received a letter to say you've missed a payment or you've got a letter about a default notice, it's important that as soon as that default has registered, you go and fix it. Pay it off, close the account and act as responsibly as possible; that's what lenders are looking to see on your credit file.

Debt to Income Ratio

One risk-based approach that lenders take is to look at an applicant's income and their total (non-mortgage) credit balance as a percentage of that income. For example, someone with an annual income of £100,000 and £25,000 of credit card balances and personal loans would have a debt-to-income ratio of 25%. Understandably, the higher that %, the higher risk the lender considers the application. Someone with a £100,000 annual income and £150,000 of outstanding loans and credit cards would represent a much higher risk to the lender of being unable to manage their finances in the future. This catches some people out who have virtually no credit card or loans outstanding; however, they have PCP car finance with low payments but a high balloon payment.

This is especially the case if both cars are in one applicant's name. It's not uncommon for Land Rover, Jaguar, BMW, etc., to have £40,000 – £80,000 balloon payments on their PCP deals. In reality, these "debts" will never have to be paid as the car will be handed back. However, some lenders have quite strict debt-to-income % rules. Someone with a perfect credit score can still be declined for a mortgage based on a high DTI ratio.

Check My File Credit Report

There are several providers of credit scores in the UK. Some are completely free of charge, and others offer free trials followed by paid subscriptions. Keeping a close eye on your credit score and report at all times is something I would highly recommend for good financial housekeeping. However, for the purposes of applying for a mortgage – the gold standard is Checkmyfile. For one simple reason – it compiles the information from all four credit reference agencies into one report. Different lenders credit search with different providers. Some lenders are open about which one(s) they use, and others do not disclose this information.

Many providers of loans, credit cards, Hire Purchase, Leases, Mortgages, and other financial agreements do not report to all four credit reference agencies. This means the data from Experian might not match Equifax and vice versa. One of the most common reasons for mortgage delays/declines is defaults from Utility Providers/Communication Providers. Credit agreements like old mobile phone contracts, electricity bills from a previous property, etc., routinely go into default for small amounts: £10 – £100 defaults from "closing balances" where the applicant has not received the final bill due to moving home or missing the email. It's not uncommon for someone to have a perfect credit score on Experian and a terrible score on Equifax. Checkmyfile provides the most comprehensive report and means that if there are any issues (known or unknown), they can be resolved or explained from the outset.

Credit Impaired

The Financial Conduct Authority's definition of a credit-impaired customer is someone who has:

(a) *within the last two years has owed overdue payments, in an amount equivalent to three months' payments, on a mortgage or other loan (whether secured or unsecured.*
(b) *has been the subject of one or more county court judgments, with a total value greater than £500, within the last three years; or*
(c) *has been subject to an individual voluntary arrangement or bankruptcy order which was in force at any time within the last three years.*

Lenders have their own internal rules on lending to borrowers who meet the definition of credit impaired, which can make accessing low interest rate borrowing much harder. It is very frustrating for both the mortgage adviser and the borrower when they have "fallen out" with a mobile phone provider or utility provider over a £50 bill and taken the "I'm not paying that" approach. This can mean having 3-4 months' worth of missed payments on an unsecured credit agreement and restricted access to prime mortgage lenders/interest rates. It is always better to pay these bills and then raise them as a dispute with the provider separately.

Chapter 10

Monthly Expenditure

What the Banks Ask

Lenders ask what your monthly expenditure on the categories below is. For a remortgage of an existing property, this is based on your current house. For a purchase of a new property, the figures have to be based on the property you are buying. Lenders will check your answers automatically against the ONS (Office for National Statistics) and use the higher of your estimates or the ONS figures. (This means there is no point in declaring you can feed a family of five for £200 per month, as the lender will not use this figure). In cases where affordability is deemed tight/you are borrowing every penny that is considered affordable by the lender, they will likely scrutinise the bank statements to confirm there is no undisclosed expenditure.

- ✓ Mortgage
- ✓ Council Tax
- ✓ Gas
- ✓ Electricity

- ✓ Oil
- ✓ Water
- ✓ Home Phone/Broadband
- ✓ Food Shopping
- ✓ Alcohol/Drinking
- ✓ Building & Contents Insurance
- ✓ Mobile Phones
- ✓ Boiler Cover/Insurance
- ✓ Prescriptions/Medication
- ✓ Petrol/Diesel
- ✓ Road Tax
- ✓ Car Insurance
- ✓ Private School Fees
- ✓ Private Medical/Insurance

Why Banks Ask

Years ago, lenders worked off relatively straightforward income multiples. If you earned £100,000 a year, you could borrow £475,000 – £550,000 based on a 4.75x to 5.5x your income multiple.

A full review was carried out by the government called the Mortgage Market Review (MMR). This review effectively concluded there was too much high-risk lending prior to 2008, and too many people could not repay the mortgages they took out when interest rates increased. The summary of that report is 185 pages long and could be the subject of a book in itself.

Some of the key things that came out of the Mortgage Market Review was that it became mandatory to get regulated advice on mortgage products either directly from the bank or via mortgage brokers. Lenders also had to introduce interest rate stress tests to ensure that borrowers would afford the monthly payments when interest rates increased in the years to come. In order to demonstrate you can afford the payments under higher interest rates, lenders are required to verify the level of disposable income you have. This effectively means that although lenders will still use "Income Multiples" to determine the max loan, they will then make deductions based on your expenditure.

A simple example of this would be a married couple with no credit cards, no loans, no car finance and no financial dependants earning £50,000 each, being able to borrow a maximum of £550,000 with several lenders. Compare this to a situation where we have a married couple with one person earning £100,000 and the other earning £0 as a homemaker. Then add in four kids, £20,000 of credit card debt, £375 per month personal loan payment and two hire purchase agreements of £400 per month each. The Mortgage Market Review, in essence, said although both these households have a gross income of £100,000, they should categorically not be able to borrow the same amount on a mortgage.

An important thing to note is that all lenders interpret the rules slightly differently, and have distinct affordability calculators. As the aim of these rules is to ensure you can afford the mortgage when interest rates increase, often you can borrow more by taking a 5-year fixed rate or longer. Lenders then know your rate will not increase for the foreseeable future.

Lenders Like Explanations: As noted previously, lenders will make certain assumptions unless you can tell them (and ideally prove to them) something to the contrary. For example, if you have three kids, lenders will make certain assumptions as to the minimum cost for childcare. You can put £0 on the mortgage application for monthly childcare costs; however, most lenders will not accept that figure. It may be that one parent works from home permanently, or there may be grandparents or other family looking after the kids during the day. Providing a clear and plausible explanation goes a long way with lenders assessing your application.

Lenders Like Proof, Not Promises: Underwriters are looking at a stack of information ranging from your credit file to your bank statements. Telling them that you will cut back spending on certain areas after buying a new house does not give them much confidence. They are looking at potentially three months' bank statements and making a determination if you will repay a £500,000 mortgage on time for the next 25 years. So, really you want those three months to be squeaky clean. E.g. more money coming in than going out, no extravagant expenditure. The underwriter needs to be comfortable that when it comes to it, you are going to pay the mortgage on time every month. Things like overdrafts being maxed out, returned direct debits and £10 in the bank the day before payday are all red flags to an underwriter that you may struggle to pay the mortgage if interest rates increase.

One of the simplest things you can do in the lead-up to applying for a mortgage on a new house is to look at the increased payments for things like the mortgage, council tax and utilities and leave that money in the bank each month. For example, let's say your current outgoings on the mortgage, council tax and utilities are £2,500 per month, and the new house will be £4,000 per month. Leaving £1,500 in the bank each month (£4,500 total in 3 months) demonstrates to an underwriter you can cut back on other expenditures and comfortably afford the new mortgage.

The mortgage market has changed massively since the Mortgage Market Review. In previous years, lenders didn't ask many questions and didn't want much, if any, proof of what you told them.

It was virtually all based on the property, with lenders taking the view that house prices will always rise and they could always repossess the property if needed. Now, they can be held responsible, and if it's deemed that they shouldn't have lent the money in the first place, they might not be able to repossess the property. They need to make sure they lend to people in the right situation to borrow, and consider people's past, present and future circumstances. Knowing that gives you an advantage. You need to understand that banks are not the enemy. They want to lend you money; they want you to pay them back and then borrow more. You need to understand that underwriters/lending managers at the banks are taught to act like it's their own money being lent. Ultimately it is; if they sanction lending to the wrong people, and the bank determines they should have declined the case, they are potentially out of a job. The aim of using an experienced mortgage broker is to put your case together to explain your circumstances and background to a mortgage lender to make it easy for them to say yes to your application.

Chapter 11

Source of Deposit, Proof of Deposit & Personal Bank Statements

What the Banks Ask

For the Deposit On the New Property – Where is the Money Coming From?

- ✓ Savings
- ✓ Non-Repayable Family Gift
- ✓ Equity from Sale of Current Property
- ✓ Inheritance
- ✓ Other? (Very Few Alternatives Are Acceptable to Lenders)

FOR Each Personal Bank Account/Savings Account You Have:

- ✓ Who's Account (Applicant 1/2/Joint)
- ✓ Sort Code
- ✓ Account Number
- ✓ Bank Name
- ✓ Overdraft Limit
- ✓ Year Account Opened
- ✓ Current Balance (+/-)

Why Banks Ask

The source of deposit and proof of deposit is often overlooked as part of the mortgage application. It's a very important part of the application and can have an impact on which lender is best placed to approach for a mortgage. This is because, like other parts of lending criteria, different banks have different views on what is considered an acceptable source of deposit funds.

Equity in Current Property: This is easy for the lender to verify. They will look for a letter from your solicitor confirming the sale price of your current property, minus your existing mortgage, which gives you a clear amount of equity in your current property to use as the deposit for the onward purchase. The lender will make a condition of the new mortgage offer that the solicitors verify this at the point of settlement. If, for whatever reason, the equity is not enough, and there has to be £10,000 from savings or a £10,000 gift from a family member, this must be declared to the lender.

Savings: If funds for the deposit are coming from your own personal savings, then lenders will want to see a minimum of 12 months of bank statements showing your savings being built up. The important thing to note is that the source of the deposit must be plausible to the lender. So, if you earn £40,000 a year and have £100,000 in savings, then lenders know, based on your after-tax income, that amount would have taken 3-4 years to save, even if you didn't have one pound of expenditure. In these cases, lenders will ask for bank statements going back longer than 12 months to identify the true source of funds or satisfy themselves the money truly is savings.

Any large credits must be explained. This could be birthday gifts from relatives, the sale of a car, or inheritance money. If it is inheritance, the lender is going to look for a letter from the solicitor to say that they acted in the estate of whoever the person that died was and how much you were entitled to as a result of that inheritance. They'll also want to see that money going from the solicitor's bank account to your bank account.

Non-Repayable Family Gift: Lenders need several things to satisfy themselves with this deposit source. A gifted deposit letter confirming the gift is fully non-repayable, the gifters will not live in the property, the gifters will not have any interest in the property or attempt to secure the money by way of a second charge in the property. Most lenders only allow immediate family (parents, grandparents and siblings. Some lenders will go as far out as uncles/aunts) to gift the deposit. It has to be plausible in relation to the overall transaction. Getting a non-repayable family gift of £20,000 – £30,000 is routine. Getting a £200,000 – £300,000 gift is a potential red flag for lenders. They are concerned that this money may, in fact, be a loan that will be paid back in the years to come. Ultimately, they will suspect that you are using that money to get around the maximum purchase price you can afford on your own. Lenders generally require an explanation of which family member is gifting the money and that they can afford to do so comfortably without any undue hardship.

Due Diligence: Lenders are doing more and more due diligence on the source of funds, so it is vital to be 100% clear with the lender where the deposit is coming from. If it is from a combination of sources, then the lender needs to see a breakdown of the different amounts, along with the corresponding proof of funds.

Personal/Family Loans as Deposit & Associated Mortgage Fraud: One of the most common areas of attempted mortgage fraud in the UK is people using personal loans or family loans as deposits.

Lenders have a real issue with this and, in 99.99% of cases, will simply decline the mortgage application if they suspect this is happening. Lenders have clear (and, for the most part, fair) rules on how much can be afforded/borrowed, and they take a very dim view of people trying to circumvent their rules by borrowing more money from other sources. The exception to this is for very small amounts of money with an even smaller collection of lenders. For example, when buying a £200,000 property and putting down a £20,000 deposit – if you only have £10,000 from savings, you will need another £12,000 for the deposit and solicitors fees. If that £12,000 personal loan is £250 per month and the lender determines you can comfortably afford the mortgage payment and the personal loan payment, then they may, on a case-by-case basis, accept the loan as part of the deposit. However, this is a minute fraction of the mortgage lenders in the UK.

Nevertheless, larger family loans and personal loans are no longer considered acceptable deposit sources. The FCA's view and the lender's view are very clear – buy a house you can afford. If you have maxed out your borrowing with the mortgage, used all your own savings and family gifts and still cannot afford the house – you simply should not be buying it. When interest rates rise and the cost of living increases each year, you may struggle to make the monthly payments or repay the family loan.

A quick note on Joint-Borrower-Sole-Proprietor Mortgages: If you have a family member with excess wealth or disposable monthly income willing to assist you in buying a property, then lenders have a product for this. It allows a second (or third/ fourth with some lenders) applicant to be added to the mortgage to boost affordability. They are not on the title deeds to the property, so there is no stamp duty impact on this. Lenders will insist that this person gets independent legal advice. Otherwise, it is a relatively straightforward product that is becoming more popular with more lenders entering the market each year.

Why Banks Ask (Bank Account Details)

Bank Account Information: Lenders want to know about each bank account you have so they can fully verify your income and expenditure. Lenders know that people routinely underestimate their monthly expenditure on mortgage applications.

Incoming Transactions: Lenders want to see the credits on the bank statements matching the amounts and dates on the payslips. They want to see a relatively consistent income for self-employed applicants, in line with the income being declared on tax returns. Lenders will always want explanations for any large one-off incoming transactions, especially in the months prior to a mortgage application.

Outgoing Transactions: Lenders need to verify your expenditure. Lenders are fully aware that people often have more than one bank account, and they want to verify the expenditure across all accounts to make sure nothing is being hidden from them. Many monthly expenses will not show on the credit searches – such as private school fees and repayment of private loans. In addition, lenders know that the credit search will not identify all credit commitments because not all lenders and credit providers report to every credit reference agency, so you have Experian, Equifax, Call Credit, and Transunion. Additionally, not all providers of credit, such as car financing, loans and overdrafts, report to all four credit reference agencies, so lenders ask you to declare any and all commitments on your application.

In recent years, car subscriptions have become more popular. Previously, when looking for a new car, you had the option of Hire Purchase/PCP/PCH or Lease etc., all of which showed up on your credit report. Now there are more providers of car subscriptions. For example, a Cazoo subscription and Land Rover/Jaguar Pivotal subscription are basically anywhere between £500 and £1,500 per month for a rolling subscription – effectively, Netflix for cars. You pay a certain amount every month, and you have access to whatever car you want from their menu. The challenge these agreements pose to mortgage lenders is often that these agreements don't show up on a credit search. This is why lenders often want three months of bank statements for all bank accounts – to ensure they are making a lending decision based on all the available information.

Exclusive Products & Auto Income Verification: Some lenders will offer you cheaper mortgage interest rates if you have a standard or premier bank account with them. Some lenders are incorporating open banking into their online mortgage applications. This basically allows them to scan through your bank account(s) digitally and determine if your income/expenditure is sufficient to afford the mortgage you need without needing additional documents or paperwork.

Savings/Offset Accounts: Having savings in the bank is a good thing when applying for a mortgage for two main reasons. Firstly, it tells the lender you are living within your means and putting money away each month for a rainy day. This is especially important in a time of increasing interest rates and the rising cost of living. Secondly, if you have a large amount of savings, it can be worth looking into the benefits of an offset mortgage. For example, if you have a £500,000 mortgage and £150,000 in savings, you only pay interest on the £350,000 difference. This can add up to a sizeable saving over the term of the mortgage.

Chapter 12

Use of New Loan Funds

What the Banks Ask

Before the banks give you hundreds of thousands/millions of pounds, they need to know exactly what you are doing with it, for example:

- ✓ Repay Existing Mortgage
- ✓ Buy a New Property
- ✓ Home Improvements
- ✓ Debt Consolidation
- ✓ Gift to a Family Member
- ✓ Business Purposes
- ✓ Other Legal Purpose

Why Banks Ask

The Financial Conduct Authority collects a monumental amount of information from mortgage lenders. Previously using a system called GABRIEL (**Ga**thering **B**etter **R**egulatory **I**nformation **Elec**tronically) and now called RegData. They want to know (amongst other things) the purpose of loan funds being used, specifically with regards to capital raising or additional funds not directly linked to the purchase price. As a result, the lenders need to know the breakdown of money being borrowed. For example, on a £500,000 loan, there may be three elements: £400,000 to repay the existing lender, £40,000 for home improvements and £60,000 for debt consolidation of unsecured debts. The FCA monitors how much lenders have lent in each different area.

It is therefore essential to be accurate with the exact breakdown of funds being raised. Most lenders require a full and detailed explanation of any additional funds being raised. For example, if you are raising money for home improvements, the lender may ask to see planning permission and quotes for the work being done. If you are consolidating other debts, the lender will want full details of the loans/credit cards and an explanation of how the debt became unmanageable or grew to the level it had to be consolidated and secured on your home. They will also want to be assured it will not happen again. Lenders regularly insist on seeing copies of planning permission and building warrants because if you carry out those improvements without the necessary paperwork, it actually detracts from the value of your property as you cannot sell or refinance the property without the correct paperwork.

In most cases, the process of getting planning permission, building warrants etc., could take 12 weeks at a minimum, so it's important you have that paperwork in place and have a breakdown of what you're using the funds for. Lenders do have discretion on what to ask for and when. If you are performing a small extension or loft conversion, they may not ask for too much information. However, if you are raising £500,000 for a massive double-height extension, they are much more interested in seeing all the paperwork, schedule of works and build cost estimates. Most importantly, they want confirmation the property will remain habitable during the building work.

If it's for capital raising to put money into the business, they're likely to ask for a letter from the accountant confirming what that money is going to be used for, how it's going to be repaid and over what term it will be repaid. They want to make sure that the business is still sustainable and viable, that you're not taking money out of your residential house to save a dying business that's going to go under in six months' time anyway. The lender doesn't want to be using their security for that to delay the inevitable. So, it's important to declare to the lender what it is that you're doing with the funds you're raising from them.

Client Case Studies

Type of Case

Remortgage + Capital Raising for Home Improvements

Valuation/Purchase Price

£1,350,000

Mortgage Amount

£700,000

Case Summary & Challenges

The clients were self-employed, minority shareholders in a family business.

They wanted to embark on a large home improvement project, including an extension.

The clients' income had increased by over 300% from one tax year to the next.

The clients' business was involved in the manufacture of PPE Equipment. Taking an average of the two years meant the mortgage was not affordable on paper. Additionally, the lenders who would look to use the most recent years' income alone were not comfortable doing so due to concerns over how sustainable the higher income would be post-pandemic. Clients had been told by a previous broker they could not get the mortgage they wanted.

Solution

We took the case to a specialist lender for the self-employed – a lender with experienced underwriters, able to look beyond the headline numbers involved. We spoke with the underwriter directly on the case and provided a detailed explanation from the company's chartered accountant. We explained that the business had been trading for over 20 years and that much of the growth in the most recent year had come from orders placed before the pandemic started. We provided management accounts and company bank statements showing the strength of the business. The underwriter agreed the income was sustainable and was happy to proceed with the case. At the end of the 2-year fixed rate, once the home improvements are complete, they will refinance to a standard high street bank.

Lender
Specialist Lender

Fixed Rate Length
2 Year Fixed Rate

Interest Rate
2.48%

Top Tips
Personal Tax Returns & Financial Year End Accounts are often produced 6 to 9 months prior to a mortgage application being submitted. As such, they can be considered "historic" by lenders. For clients with complex incomes, a letter from the company accountant explaining the accounts and providing up-to-date management accounts with commentary on how the business is doing now often helps the underwriter feel more comfortable about agreeing to issue a mortgage offer on a case.

Type of Case
New House Purchase

Valuation/Purchase Price
£1,450,000

Mortgage Amount
£1,075,000

Case Summary & Challenges
The client worked for a large family business which had recently completely restructured.
Previously, the business was one limited company selling many different types of products to various industries. The business was restructured to have a Parent/Holding company at the top, with several subsidiary companies trading under different names and from various locations. The client took a salary from one of the subsidiary companies where he was involved in the day-to-day operations; the rest of the income was from dividends from the parent company. Although the salary and dividends were in excess of £100K, the client needed a mortgage well over the traditional maximum of 5.5x income.

Solution
We discussed the case at length with our contact at the large loans team of a high street bank that handles mortgages over £1 million. Although the client's salary and dividends were £100K, the client's entitlement to profits was far higher; however, the majority of profits were reinvested in the company. The client had an entitlement closer to £400K in profits in the most recent year, and the bank was happy to lend on the strength of those profits.

Lender
High Street Bank

Fixed Rate Length
5 Year Fixed Rate

Interest Rate
1.14%

Top Tips
Every lender calculates income slightly differently for self-employed applicants.
Lending based on using Salary + Share of profit before/after tax is very unique.

Type of Case
Remortgage of a Self-Build Property

Valuation/Purchase Price
£1,200,000

Mortgage Amount
£720,000

Case Summary & Challenges
The client had a custom-built property which had recently been completed. He also had his current family home, which he planned to sell within the next two years. The client used his own savings to build the property, which he originally planned to replenish with the sale of his current property. In order to achieve the maximum sale price on the current property, it required upgrading and modernisation. The client also needed funds to help one of his children get onto the property ladder, and help another build their own home. On paper, he could not afford two mortgages. In addition, his son wanted to live in the current property until his self-build property was also constructed. The client's existing mortgage lender was not interested in lending more funds due to the nature of the client's income and the fact it would be a second home.

Solution
The client needed a lender willing to take a common sense approach to the four separate complexities of the case:

1) It was a custom-built property from a small builder.
2) It would not be the client's only residence.

3) The client's salary + dividend income were not sufficient, so the lender needed to factor in retained earnings when deciding how much to lend.
4) The client was raising a lot of money, for various different reasons, including gifting to children and repaying debts associated with the cost of building the house.

The case was discussed at length with the underwriter, who was given a full explanation of the client's circumstances, including the long-term plans for both properties. They were happy with the client's intentions and ability to repay the mortgage and proceeded to issue the mortgage offer.

Lender
High Street Bank

Fixed Rate Length
5 Year Fixed

Interest Rate
1.29%

Top Tips
Before embarking on a self-build project, it is often substantially more cost-effective to sell your current property, release the equity and move into rented accommodation for 12-18 months during the build. Cash flow during these projects is vital.

Type of Case
Remortgage

Valuation/Purchase Price
£1,100,000

Mortgage Amount
£570,000

Case Summary & Challenges
The client was with a specialist lender, having completed a full renovation of his property. The current lender did not offer product transfers or rate switches, so the client was stuck paying a high standard variable rate whilst trying to refinance to a new lender. The challenge was the client was self-employed, and the business had a really tough time during the pandemic. Turnover was down, costs were up, and profit dropped considerably, meaning the client's share of the profits was non-existent compared to previous years. On paper, he couldn't afford to borrow anything close to what he needed to repay his current mortgage lender.

Solution
We took the time to prepare a detailed summary for potential lenders, to get the case pre-approved prior to submitting a formal application. We explained that the business had been trading through economic peaks and troughs for over 20 years. We provided three years of accounts for previous years, a detailed explanation of how the pandemic had impacted the client's industry. Then, we provided management accounts for the current financial year along with business bank statements showing that the business was recovering well. We demonstrated how the client had been able to take dividends

all the way through the pandemic due to having retained significant earnings in the company. We could prove that in the previous healthy years of trading, the client left a lot of his profits within the business. Due to their "saving for a rainy day" mentality, the client survived the pandemic and picked up trading as normal. We persuaded a high street bank to accept the case and issue a mortgage offer.

Lender
High Street Bank

Fixed Rate Length
5 Year Fixed

Interest Rate
1.34%

Top Tips
Lenders can take a common sense view on many things if they are given all the information and proper explanations. Ultimately, they need to be certain of your ability to repay the loan.

Type of Case
Purchase (Joint-Borrower-Sole-Proprietor)

Valuation/Purchase Price
£600,000

Mortgage Amount
£510,000

Case Summary & Challenges
The primary client was a first-time buyer, had saved a sizeable deposit and had some non-repayable family gifts towards the deposit from grandparents wishing to help him buy his first house. The client had done his own research and worked out the monthly payment for the mortgage he would need using an online mortgage payment calculator.

The client viewed a house he liked, put an offer in on the property and it was accepted.

The client then realised that lenders had a maximum income multiple, and despite being able to afford the monthly payments, no lender would lend him anywhere near the amount he needed to borrow to buy the house. The client was then advised to speak to a mortgage broker to determine if there were any other options available to him.

Solution
The client could comfortably afford the mortgage; in reality, he had no debt and was very conservative with his spending. The client worked in an industry where it was a fair assumption his earnings would continue to rise at a decent level. The client did not want to buy a smaller house, and have the costs and hassle of moving again

in a few years when his wages were at a level deemed necessary by the banks to justify the mortgage amount.
We arranged a Joint-Borrower-Sole-Proprietor Mortgage, which involved adding his father to the application and using his surplus income to support the application. The father was on the mortgage but not the title deeds to the property, so there was no impact on stamp duty. In two years, the client will simply remortgage into his own name only and remove his father from the mortgage application. This is a little-known solution which can help first-time buyers.

Lender
Specialist Bank

Fixed Rate Length
2 Year Fixed

Interest Rate
2.79%

Type of Case
Day 1 Remortgage (Property Bought Cash)

Valuation/Purchase Price
£800,000

Mortgage Amount
£555,000

Case Summary & Challenges
The client identified a property which he wanted to buy. This was several weeks before the end of the "Stamp Duty Holiday" in June 2021. The mortgage market was exceptionally busy, and there was no chance of his application being completed in time to buy the property with a mortgage. The client sold his previous property and funded the shortfall with a short-term loan from his family in order to complete the purchase before the end of the stamp duty holiday. The client had been (wrongly!) advised he would need to wait six months before any lender would allow him to remortgage the property. His family were prepared to wait for their money back; however, the property needed renovations and improvements prior to being ready to move into. The client wanted to know if any lender would consider lending within six months.

Solution
Several high street banks offer "Day 1 Remortgages"; however, the vast majority need the property to be owned for six months. We recommended a high street bank who has happy to refinance straight away to repay a family loan. The bank just had to be comfortable with the original source of funds used for the purchase and the use of the additional funds being raised. We got the client a free valua-

tion, free legal work and a mortgage offer within a few weeks of the original purchase. The client's family were out of pocket for less than a month.

Lender
High Street Bank

Fixed Rate Length
2 Years

Interest Rate
1.21%

Type of Case
Purchase

Valuation/Purchase Price
£750,000

Mortgage Amount
£525,000

Case Summary & Challenges
The clients had viewed a property they liked and made an offer which was accepted. The clients assumed they would have no problems obtaining a mortgage for the desired amount; however, they had been "max loaned" by their banks, who determined they could not afford to borrow the amount they wanted. This was because both clients worked in sales with a relatively low basic salary and a high amount of commission on bonuses. This income varied considerably from month to month. In some months, commission was £5k; in others, it was only £500. Both clients had been in their current roles for just over one year and did not have the 2-3-year track record of P60s to show the income was sustainable that their existing bank required. They were told they needed a much larger deposit, which they could not manage.

Solution
The clients provided 12 months of payslips and 12 months of bank statements. We evidenced to the lender that the basic income and even the minimum commission received one month was more than sufficient to pay the mortgage and household bills. We demonstrated to the lender that the clients had been saving more than half their net pay consistently for 12 months to raise the deposit for the

property. We showed that the clients were responsible and conservative with their money, had no debt and owned their cars outright. The bank agreed that, although the mortgage amount was out with their standard criteria, the clients were low risk and proceeded to offer the loan anyway.

Lender
High Street Bank

Fixed Rate Length
5 Year Fixed

Interest Rate
1.68%

Type of Case
Purchase

Valuation/Purchase Price
£1,175,500

Mortgage Amount
£780,000

Case Summary & Challenges
The client agreed to a purchase price on a new family home. The challenge was the sellers had several previous sales fall through due to the chain collapsing. They were not prepared to accept an offer from anyone who still had a house to sell. As a result, my client agreed to buy the property not "subject to sale of his existing property." The client came to me looking for a bridging loan to buy the property, which, albeit available, was incredibly expensive in terms of interest rate and fees. A bridging loan would also have meant refinancing later.

Solution
We took the time to understand the client's income and expenditure as well as their share in the family business. However, the client's salary and dividends alone were insufficient to support the mortgage on his existing property plus a new property. The family business was doing very well, had large cash reserves, and the directors routinely left the majority of the profits invested in the business. The solution was to speak to the large loans team of a high street bank and demonstrate the client needed a decent long-term mortgage on the new property. He would be selling his existing property and redeeming the mortgage as soon as possible, so the timeframe of

having two properties would be relatively short. The underwriter was satisfied with the client's intentions and issued the mortgage offer for the new property without making it a condition that the current mortgage was redeemed first. This allowed the client to lock in an excellent long-term fixed rate and save nearly £60,000 in interest in fees which would have been payable for a huge bridging loan. The client saved a small fortune and got his new house.

Lender
High Street Bank

Fixed Rate Length
5 Years

Interest Rate
1.14%

A lifeline for a self-employed single mum

Background:

Denise is a self-employed single mum working as a taxi driver. She was looking to move house with a 95% loan to value mortgage, so she could have an extra room for her growing family but remain on the same street close to her Dad.

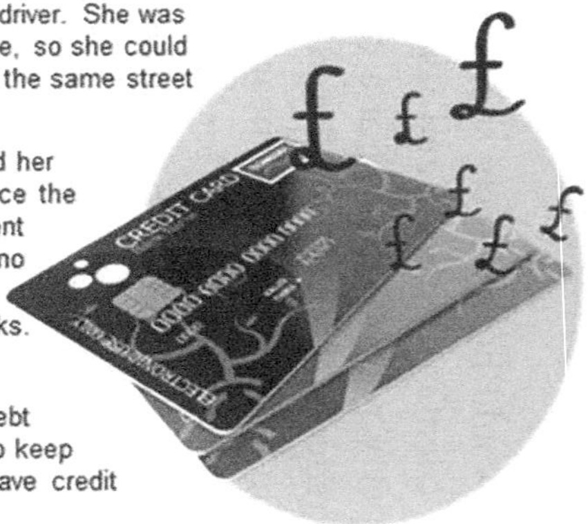

Denise had poor credit history after a messy divorce, and her credit cards were maxed out. She was struggling to service the high interest rates on the debt but had not done any recent additional borrowing or spending on the cards. She had no late payments or defaults within the last three years, however, she was refused mortgages by high street banks.

Aldermore solution:

Denise took a secured loan out to repay all credit card debt and reduce monthly payments. Her broker advised her to keep the cards open to demonstrate to Aldermore she could have credit available but not use it.

Denise was able to show three years of accounts to prove affordability and increases in earnings during that period to show she could sustain repayments and be prepared in case of any future increases in her monthly costs. Denise also provided the broker with 12 months worth of bank statements, and the Aldermore underwriter went through all 110 pages of it to assess if Denise's income was consistent, sustainable and accurate (along with chartered accountant reference).

Aldermore then were able to offer a 95% loan to value mortgage, with a monthly payment considerably less than the previous mortgage and debt payments.

"I advised her to leave all the credit cards open to demonstrate to Aldermore that she could have credit available and not use it – this boosted her credit score, but not enough for high street banks to even look at the case."

Robert Moffat
St Clair Financial Planning

Aldermore

A leg-up onto the ladder for a 28-year old car salesman

Background:

Darren is a 28 year old first time buyer, who lived at home and was gifted a deposit from a family member. He tried but failed to get a mortgage with a high street bank. He approached other smaller lenders but they wouldn't help him borrow on a flat, and the deposit he had meant he couldn't borrow at the loan-to-value he needed.

Darren had zero credit history due to having a company car, living at home with no bills and no debt. He also had a low basic income working in sales, but earned decent commission.

Aldermore solution:

Darren came to Aldermore who were able to dig into the detail of his finances, and understand his low basic income but high commission on sales meant he could afford and sustain repayments on a mortgage. The broker also was able to show Aldermore 5 months of banking statements to prove, while he had no credit history, he was responsible in his spending and saving regularly for solicitor fee's, decorating and furniture etc.

This satisfied Aldermore's underwriter and Darren had a 95% loan-to-value mortgage approved with Aldermore, and was given advice from Aldermore and his broker on how to build up a good credit rating for the future.

"The applicant has been saving for the last 5 months (since being given a stern word by myself for the amount of money wasted eating out and recreation) and the bank statements showed he had consistently saved more than the new mortgage payment each month."

Robert Moffat
St Clair Financial Planning

About the Author

Robert Moffat is a Specialist Mortgage Adviser with over ten years of experience in residential mortgage advice.

He studied in Glasgow, graduating with a Bachelor of Arts in Finance, Investment and Risk. Subsequently, Robert achieved the following qualifications at the London Institute of Banking and Finance: Certificate in Mortgage Advice (CeMAP), Certificate in Equity Release (CeRER), Certificate in Long Term Care Provision (CertLTCP), Diploma in Financial Planning (DipFA) and Diploma in Mortgage Advice (DipMAP). Robert is currently completing his Advanced Diploma in Financial Planning (AdvDipFA).

Robert is a Member of the London Institute of Banking and Finance (MLIBF).

Robert specialises in mortgage advice for people who are self-employed or have complex incomes, including directors of ltd companies, minority shareholders in family businesses, partnerships, contract workers, and sole traders, to name a few.

Throughout his extensive experience, Robert has supported many clients encountering complicated challenges when trying to obtain mortgages. Hence, he has written this book to explain some of the difficulties self-employed people or those with complex incomes face and how to overcome them.

Made in the USA
Monee, IL
04 November 2026

67379698R00059